Animal Migrations

Insect Migration

by Shannon Anderson

FOCUS READERS

BEACON

www.focusreaders.com

Focus Readers is distributed by North Star Editions:
sales@northstareditions.com | 888-417-0195

Produced for Focus Readers by Red Line Editorial.

Photographs ©: Shutterstock Images, cover, 1, 4, 7, 8, 11, 14–15, 16, 19, 20, 22, 25, 29; Red Line Editorial, 13; iStockphoto, 27

Library of Congress Cataloging-in-Publication Data
Names: Anderson, Shannon, 1972- author.
Title: Insect migration / by Shannon Anderson.
Description: Lake Elmo, MN : Focus Readers, [2024] | Series: Animal
   migrations | Includes index. | Audience: Grades 2-3
Identifiers: LCCN 2022055004 (print) | LCCN 2022055005 (ebook) | ISBN
   9781637396087 (hardcover) | ISBN 9781637396650 (paperback) | ISBN
   9781637397763 (ebook pdf) | ISBN 9781637397220 (hosted ebook)
Subjects: LCSH: Insects--Migration--Juvenile literature.
Classification: LCC QL496.2 .A53 2024 (print) | LCC QL496.2 (ebook) | DDC
   595.7156/8--dc23/eng/20221209
LC record available at https://lccn.loc.gov/2022055004
LC ebook record available at https://lccn.loc.gov/2022055005

Printed in the United States of America
Mankato, MN
082023

About the Author

Shannon Anderson is an award-winning author and educator who lives in Indiana with her family and many pets. She enjoys sharing her love of reading, writing, and learning through author visits.

Table of Contents

Chapter 1

Monarchs on the Move

Every spring, huge swarms of monarch butterflies leave Mexico. The beautiful insects fly north. They are beginning a long journey. Soon, the monarchs find milkweed plants. They lay eggs on the leaves.

 Huge groups of monarch butterflies gather in Mexico before leaving.

The eggs hatch. Caterpillars come out. They spend two weeks eating milkweed leaves. Next, each caterpillar forms a **chrysalis**.

The caterpillars stay in their hard cases for about 10 days. When they come out, they are butterflies. They continue the trip north.

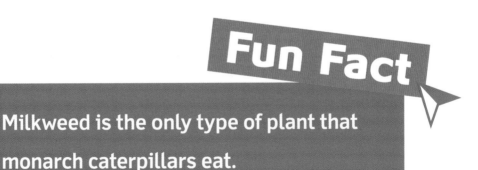

Fun Fact

Milkweed is the only type of plant that monarch caterpillars eat.

 Monarch butterflies use the position of the sun to find their way.

The new monarchs lay the next batch of eggs. After two months, a third or fourth **generation** reaches Canada. In the fall, the monarchs will begin flying back to Mexico.

Chapter 2

One-Way Migration

Many insects fly to other areas to lay their eggs. However, some insects have short lives. They do not live long enough to fly back. This is known as one-way **migration**.

The desert locust is a type of grasshopper. It makes one-way migrations.

Desert locusts have one-way migration. They live in Africa and parts of Asia. After heavy rains, desert locusts lay their eggs. Millions of baby locusts are born. Before long, they run out of food. So, they move to other areas. They seek more food. They also seek new areas to lay their eggs.

Desert locusts migrate in huge swarms. Millions of them fly together. They travel up to 80 miles (130 km) each day. As they move,

 Locusts have longer wings during the migration stage of their lives. This helps them fly farther.

locusts cause major damage to crops. That can lead to food shortages for people.

Painted lady butterflies also have one-way migration. These insects live in many parts of the world.

They travel to find specific flowers. For instance, they may fly from Africa to Europe. They arrive as the flowers begin to bloom. Painted ladies live for only a few weeks. So, it can take up to six generations to complete the trip.

Hoverflies also live in many parts of the world. Billions of hoverflies

Fun Fact

Painted ladies have the longest migration of any butterfly.

Migration Map

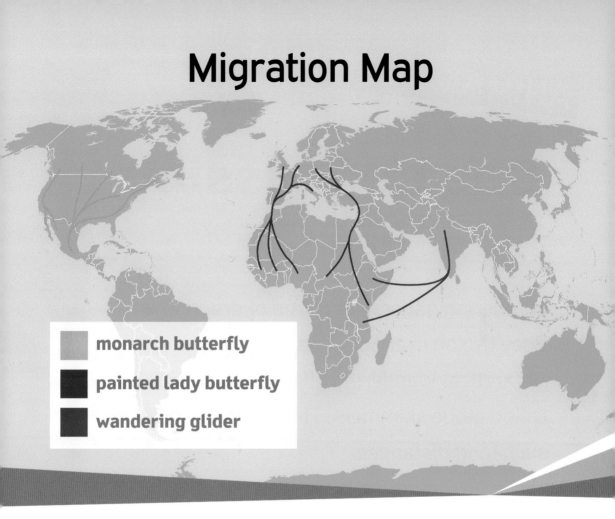

monarch butterfly

painted lady butterfly

wandering glider

migrate each winter. They spread
pollen as they move from flower
to flower. That helps crops grow.
Hoverflies also eat aphids. These
insects harm farmers' crops.

Ocean-Crossing Insects

Wandering gliders are a type of dragonfly. They live on every continent except Antarctica. Wandering gliders are sometimes called globe skimmers. That's because they fly such long distances.

Some wandering gliders migrate across an ocean. They fly all the way from India to Africa. Then they fly back to India. The wind carries the dragonflies for much of the journey. They **breed** along the way. They lay eggs in the water. It takes several generations to make the trip.

Wandering gliders can travel thousands of miles.

Chapter 3

From Breeding to Feeding

Some insects travel back and forth during their lives. They lay their eggs in one area. Then they need to find food. So, they leave their breeding area. They fly to a feeding area.

 Salt marsh mosquitoes fly back and forth between breeding areas and feeding areas.

One example is salt marsh mosquitoes. These mosquitos lay eggs in the mud around salt marshes. After the babies hatch, they leave to find food. They bite **mammals** such as horses and cows. The mosquitoes feed on their blood. In time, they are ready to lay eggs. To do so, they return to the salt marshes.

Some grasshoppers lay eggs in sand and weeds. When the eggs hatch, the babies are called

 The migratory grasshopper can be found through much of North America.

nymphs. The nymphs grow wings as they get older. They fly in swarms to find plants to eat. These swarms can cause major problems for farmers.

 Adult cockchafer beetles feed on leaves and flowers.

The cockchafer beetle lays its eggs in soil. When the eggs hatch, the **grubs** live underground. They stay there for three to four years. The grubs eat the roots of plants. They come out of the ground as adults. Then they migrate together. They go to forests to **mate**. After that, they travel again to feeding areas. Finally, the females go back to the soil and lay eggs.

Fun Fact

Cockchafer beetles have fan-like antennae. These antennae help the beetles sense their surroundings.

Chapter 4

Migrating to Hibernate

Some insects migrate to find places where they can **hibernate**. An insect's body slows down when it hibernates. That way, the insect can get through a season that is too hot or too cold.

 When convergent ladybugs hibernate, they gather in groups of up to 30 million.

Some ladybugs hibernate. Their eggs hatch in the spring. In early summer, the ladybugs become adults. They migrate to the mountains. There, they gather in groups until the rainy season begins. In the fall, they fly together to forest areas. They hibernate through the winter. In the spring, the cycle begins again.

Green darner dragonflies lay eggs in ponds. The baby dragonflies may do different things. It depends on

> Green darners are one of the most common dragonflies in North America.

the time of year. If the weather is warm, they will migrate. If it is cold, they will hibernate. It usually takes three generations of dragonflies to make their complete migration.

The first generation goes north. The second batch heads south. The third goes back north.

Bogong caterpillars live in southern Australia. Summers there can be hot and dry. So, when the caterpillars become moths, they migrate to the mountains. They find

Fun Fact

Some swarms of ladybugs and dragonflies are huge. They can show up on weather **radar.**

> The bogong moth was listed as an endangered species in 2021.

caves that are cool. They hibernate in the caves during the summer. Then, before winter comes, they fly back. They mate and lay eggs.

FOCUS ON
Insect Migration

Write your answers on a separate piece of paper.

1. Write a sentence that explains the main ideas of Chapter 2.

2. Which insect do you think has the most impressive migration? Why?

3. What kind of insect lays its eggs on milkweed plants?
   - **A.** wandering glider
   - **B.** monarch butterfly
   - **C.** desert locust

4. What would happen if hoverflies did not eat aphids?
   - **A.** Many crops would be destroyed.
   - **B.** Farmers would be able to grow more crops.
   - **C.** Farmers' crops would not be affected.

5. What does **swarms** mean in this book?

*Every spring, huge **swarms** of monarch butterflies leave Mexico. The beautiful insects fly north.*

    A. insects without wings

    B. nests where insects live

    C. large groups of insects

6. What does **cycle** mean in this book?

*In the fall, they fly together to forest areas. They hibernate through the winter. In the spring, the **cycle** begins again.*

    A. a time of cold weather

    B. a set of events that repeats

    C. a group of very big trees

Answer key on page 32.

Glossary

breed
To have babies.

chrysalis
A hard case that holds an insect that is changing into an adult.

generation
A group of people or animals born around the same time.

grubs
Soft, worm-like insects that are in the early stage of their lives.

hibernate
To save energy by resting or sleeping during a season.

mammals
Animals that have hair and produce milk for their young.

mate
To come together in order to have babies.

migration
The movement of a group of animals from one place to another.

nymphs
Insects that are in the early stage of their lives.

pollen
A powder produced by some plants that helps create new plants.

radar
A device that locates things by bouncing radio waves off them.

To Learn More

BOOKS

Huddleston, Emma. *Beneficial Insects: Bugs Helping Plants Survive*. Minneapolis: Abdo Publishing, 2020.

Huddleston, Emma. *Tiger Mosquitoes*. Lake Elmo, MN: Focus Readers, 2022.

Markle, Sandra. *Locusts: An Augmented Reality Experience*. Minneapolis: Lerner Publications, 2021.

NOTE TO EDUCATORS

Visit **www.focusreaders.com** to find lesson plans, activities, links, and other resources related to this title.

Index

Answer Key: 1. Answers will vary; **2.** Answers will vary; **3.** B; **4.** A; **5.** C; **6.** B